INDIA'S POLITICAL SAGA

JOURNEY FROM THE BEGINNING

SANDIP NAYAK

Contents

Prologue

Politics in India has always been a dynamic and multifaceted entity, constantly evolving and adapting to the changing socio-economic, cultural, and technological landscape. Since gaining independence in 1947, India has witnessed a remarkable transformation in its political landscape, from the early days of nation-building to the complexities of a modern, globalized democracy. This book aims to delve into the fascinating journey of Indian politics, exploring the key events, ideologies, and personalities that have shaped its trajectory from the dawn of independence to the present day.

CHAPTER ONE

The Dawn of Independence (1947-1950)

The Struggle for Independence:

The struggle for India's independence from British colonial rule was a defining chapter in the nation's history, marked by a combination of mass movements, civil disobedience, and non-violent resistance. It was a saga of perseverance, sacrifice, and unwavering determination led by visionary leaders such as Mahatma Gandhi, Jawaharlal Nehru, and Sardar Patel.

The Seeds of Dissent: The roots of India's freedom struggle can be traced back to the 19th century, with the rise of socio-religious reform movements like the Brahmo Samaj and Arya Samaj, which sought to challenge the oppressive practices of British colonial rule and promote social reform and nationalism. Intellectuals like Raja Ram Mohan Roy and Swami Vivekananda played pivotal roles in awakening national consciousness and fostering a sense of pride in India's cultural heritage.

Early Movements and Leaders: The early decades of the 20th century saw the emergence of political organizations such as the Indian National Congress (INC), which provided a platform for Indians to voice their grievances and demand political reforms. Leaders like Bal Gangadhar Tilak, Lala Lajpat Rai, and Bipin Chandra Pal advocated for swaraj (self-rule) and launched mass agitations against British policies such as the partition of Bengal and the Rowlatt Act.

Gandhi's Leadership and Non-Cooperation: Mahatma Gandhi's entry into the freedom struggle in the 1910s transformed the movement with his philosophy of non-violent resistance or satyagraha. The Non-Cooperation Movement of 1920-22 marked a turning point in the struggle, as millions of Indians boycotted British institutions, refused to pay taxes, and engaged in acts of civil disobedience. Despite the movement's suspension following the Chauri Chaura incident, Gandhi's methods had inspired a new generation of nationalists.

Civil Disobedience and Salt Satyagraha: The Civil Disobedience Movement launched in 1930 further intensified the struggle, with Gandhi leading the iconic Salt March to Dandi to protest against the British monopoly on salt production. Thousands joined Gandhi in defying the salt laws, symbolizing the power of non-violent resistance and civil disobedience. The movement sparked widespread protests across India, leading to mass arrests and acts of repression by the British authorities.

Quit India Movement and Independence: The Quit India Movement of 1942 marked the climax of the freedom struggle, with the INC demanding an end to British rule and the establishment of a sovereign Indian government. The movement saw widespread protests, strikes, and acts of sabotage, leading to a crackdown by the British government and the imprisonment of top leaders, including Gandhi. Despite the suppression, the movement galvanized public opinion and laid the groundwork for India's eventual independence.

Partition and Freedom: India's long and arduous struggle for independence finally bore fruit on August 15, 1947, when the British relinquished control and India was partitioned into two independent nations, India and Pakistan. While the attainment of independence was a momentous occasion, it was also marred by communal violence and the displacement of millions of people. Nonetheless, it marked the culmination of decades of sacrifice and struggle, as India embarked on a new journey as a sovereign nation.

The struggle for independence was not just a quest for political sovereignty but also a reaffirmation of India's identity, unity, and aspirations for a just and equitable society. It laid the foundation for the democratic ideals and values that continue to guide India's journey as a modern nation-state, inspiring movements for freedom and justice around the world.

The Framing of the Indian Constitution:

The process of framing the Indian Constitution was a monumental undertaking that reflected the aspirations, values, and diversity of the newly independent nation. Led by the Constituent Assembly, composed of representatives from across the country and representing various communities, religions, and ideologies, the framing of the Constitution was a historic endeavor aimed at laying the foundation for India's democratic governance.

Formation of the Constituent Assembly: The Constituent Assembly was established in December 1946, with the objective of drafting a constitution for independent India. It comprised 389 members, including prominent leaders such as Dr. B.R. Ambedkar, Jawaharlal Nehru, Sardar Patel, Rajendra Prasad, and Sarojini Naidu, representing different political parties, regions, and interest groups. The Assembly reflected the diversity of India and sought to accommodate the interests and concerns of all sections of society.

Principles and Ideals: The framing of the Indian Constitution was guided by a set of principles and ideals that reflected the aspirations of the freedom struggle and the values of justice, equality, liberty, and fraternity. Drawing inspiration from various sources, including the constitutions of other nations, the Assembly sought to create a document that would guarantee fundamental rights, protect minority rights, and establish a democratic and secular polity. The Preamble to the Constitution, which proclaims India as a sovereign, socialist, secular, and democratic republic, encapsulates the core values and objectives of the Constitution.

Drafting Committees and Committees: To facilitate the drafting process, several committees and sub-committees were constituted by the Constituent Assembly. The Drafting Committee, chaired by Dr. B.R. Ambedkar, played a central role in preparing the initial draft of the Constitution. It deliberated on various provisions, incorporating inputs from members of the Assembly and legal experts. Other committees, such as the Fundamental Rights Sub-Committee, Directive Principles Committee, and Union Powers Committee, were tasked with examining specific aspects of the Constitution and making recommendations.

Deliberations and Debates: The framing of the Constitution involved extensive deliberations and debates on key issues such as federalism, citizenship, fundamental rights, and the distribution of powers between the center and the states. Members of the Constituent Assembly engaged in spirited discussions, expressing diverse viewpoints and negotiating compromises to arrive at consensus-based decisions. The debates reflected the complexities of India's socio-political landscape and the challenges of reconciling competing interests and aspirations.

Adoption and Enactment: After nearly three years of deliberations, the Constituent Assembly adopted the final draft of the Constitution on November 26, 1949. The adoption of the Constitution marked a historic moment in India's journey as an independent nation, symbolizing the triumph of democracy, pluralism, and constitutionalism. The Constitution came into effect on January 26, 1950, replacing the Government of India Act 1935 and heralding the birth of the Republic of India. January 26th is celebrated annually as Republic Day, commemorating the adoption of the Constitution.

Legacy and Impact: The Indian Constitution stands as a testament to the vision, wisdom, and foresight of the framers, who sought to create a framework for governance that would endure the test of time. Over the years, the Constitution has been amended to address changing socio-economic and political realities, while upholding its core principles and values. It has served as a bulwark against authoritarianism, discrimination, and injustice, empowering citizens and institutions to uphold the rule of law and promote inclusive development.

Challenges of Partition and Integration

The partition of British India in 1947 into the independent nations of India and Pakistan was accompanied by immense challenges, including communal violence, mass displacement of populations, and the integration of princely states. The aftermath of partition left a profound impact on the socio-political fabric of both countries and posed significant hurdles to the task of nation-building.

Communal Violence and Displacement: Partition resulted in one of the largest mass migrations in human history, as millions of Hindus, Muslims, and Sikhs were uprooted from their homes and forced to flee to the newly formed India or Pakistan. The communal violence that erupted during partition led to widespread atrocities, including massacres, rape, and arson, leaving scars that would haunt generations to come. The trauma of displacement and the loss of lives and livelihoods created deep-seated animosities and distrust between communities, exacerbating communal tensions.

Integration of Princely States: One of the challenges facing the newly independent India was the integration of over 500 princely states, which enjoyed varying degrees of autonomy under British suzerainty. The accession of these states to either India or Pakistan was a complex process, fraught with political negotiations, diplomatic maneuvering, and occasional use of force. While most princely states acceded to India voluntarily, some, notably Hyderabad, Junagadh, and Kashmir, became flashpoints of conflict, leading to military intervention and the eventual integration into the Indian Union.

Refugee Rehabilitation and Resettlement: The partition of India resulted in the displacement of an estimated 10-15 million people, leading to a humanitarian crisis of unprecedented proportions. Refugee camps were set up across India to provide shelter, food, and medical assistance to the displaced populations, many of whom had lost everything they owned. The task of rehabilitating and resettling the refugees posed a formidable challenge to the newly independent Indian government, straining its resources and administrative capacity.

Economic Dislocation and Resource Allocation: Partition led to the division of economic assets, infrastructure, and resources between India and Pakistan, further complicating the process of nation-building. Disputes arose over the allocation of resources such as water, electricity, and irrigation facilities, leading to tensions and conflicts between the two nations. The economic dislocation caused by partition, coupled with the challenges of post-war reconstruction and development, posed formidable challenges to the nascent economies of both India and Pakistan.

Social and Cultural Reconciliation: Partition not only divided geographical boundaries but also fractured social and cultural ties that had existed for centuries. The legacy of partition continues to shape the identity and consciousness of communities on both sides of the border, influencing politics, literature, art, and popular culture. Efforts to promote reconciliation, dialogue, and people-to-people exchanges have been hampered by persistent political tensions and historical grievances, underscoring the complexity and sensitivity of the partition legacy.

The challenges of partition and integration posed formidable obstacles to the task of nation-building in post-independence India. While the wounds of partition continue to linger, India has made significant strides in overcoming the legacy of division and building a pluralistic, democratic society that celebrates diversity and inclusivity. However, the scars of partition serve as a poignant reminder of the importance of fostering harmony, tolerance, and understanding in the pursuit of a peaceful and prosperous future.

CHAPTER TWO

Nehruvian Era and Socialist Ideals (1950-1964)

Nehru's vision of a secular, socialist India and the implementation of Five-Year Plans.

Jawaharlal Nehru, India's first Prime Minister, played a pivotal role in shaping the country's political, social, and economic landscape in the years following independence. Nehru's vision for India was deeply influenced by his commitment to secularism, socialism, and democracy, which he believed were essential for building a modern and equitable society.

Secularism: Nehru envisioned India as a secular nation, where the state would remain neutral in matters of religion and uphold the principles of religious freedom, equality, and tolerance. He firmly believed in the idea of India as a multi-religious and pluralistic society, where individuals of all faiths would coexist peacefully and contribute to the nation's progress. Nehru's commitment to secularism was reflected in the preamble to the Indian Constitution, which declares India as a secular republic, as well as in his government's policies of non-interference in religious affairs and promotion of communal harmony.

Socialism: Nehru was deeply influenced by socialist ideals and believed in the need for economic planning and state intervention to address the socio-economic inequalities inherited from colonial rule. He saw socialism as a means to achieve social justice, equality, and the welfare of the masses. Nehru's government pursued a policy of mixed economy, with a combination of state-owned enterprises and private sector participation. Key sectors such as industry, agriculture, and infrastructure were nationalized or regulated to promote economic development and social welfare. The Industrial Policy Resolution of 1956, which emphasized state control over key industries and strategic sectors, was a cornerstone of Nehru's socialist agenda.

Democratic Governance: Nehru was a staunch advocate of democracy and believed in the importance of democratic institutions, processes, and values in ensuring political stability, accountability, and participation. He laid the foundations of India's parliamentary democracy, with its emphasis on free and fair elections, multi-party competition, and the rule of law. Nehru's government prioritized the establishment of democratic institutions such as the Election Commission, the Judiciary, and the Civil Services, which were essential for upholding the principles of democracy and ensuring checks and balances on executive power.

Implementation of Five-Year Plans:

In line with Nehru's vision of socialist development, India adopted a series of Five-Year Plans to guide its economic growth and development. Inspired by the Soviet model of planned economy, the Five-Year Plans aimed at achieving rapid industrialization, agricultural growth, and social welfare through centralized planning and state intervention.

First Five-Year Plan (1951-1956): The First Five-Year Plan focused on laying the foundations of industrialization and infrastructure development, with an emphasis on key sectors such as steel, coal, and power. The plan aimed at achieving a balanced growth of the economy, reducing regional disparities, and promoting employment generation and poverty alleviation. Significant investments were made in the public sector, with the establishment of major industrial projects such as the Bhilai Steel Plant and the Damodar Valley Corporation.

Second Five-Year Plan (1956-1961): The Second Five-Year Plan continued the emphasis on industrialization and infrastructure development, with a focus on heavy industries, capital goods production, and scientific research. The plan also prioritized agricultural modernization and land reforms, with the aim of increasing agricultural productivity and rural incomes. Despite facing challenges such as food shortages and inflation, the plan laid the groundwork for sustained economic growth and development in the years to come.

Subsequent Plans: Subsequent Five-Year Plans continued to prioritize industrialization, infrastructure development, and social welfare, with a focus on sectors such as education, healthcare, and rural development. The plans also emphasized the importance of self-reliance, technological innovation, and human resource development in achieving sustainable development goals. However, the efficacy of the planning process came under scrutiny due to issues such as bureaucratic inefficiency, resource constraints, and external shocks such as wars and global economic downturns.

The Non-Aligned Movement and India's role in international politics.

The Non-Aligned Movement emerged in the context of the Cold War as a coalition of states seeking to maintain their independence from the two superpower blocs led by the United States and the Soviet Union. India, under the leadership of Prime Minister Jawaharlal Nehru, played a crucial role in the formation and development of the NAM, advocating for a principled and neutral foreign policy based on the principles of non-alignment, sovereignty, and peaceful coexistence.

Origins of the Non-Aligned Movement: The Non-Aligned Movement was formally established during the Bandung Conference in 1955, which brought together leaders from newly independent Asian and African countries to discuss issues of mutual concern. The conference laid the groundwork for a new approach to international relations based on the principles of non-alignment, anti-colonialism, and anti-imperialism. India, along with other founding members such as Egypt, Yugoslavia, and Indonesia, played a key role in articulating the goals and objectives of the movement.

Principles of Non-Alignment: Non-alignment, as articulated by Nehru and other leaders of the NAM, was based on the principle of maintaining independence and autonomy in foreign policy decision-making, free from the influence or coercion of major powers. Non-aligned countries sought to pursue their national interests through diplomacy, dialogue, and cooperation, rather than alignment with either the Western or Eastern blocs. The NAM advocated for peaceful resolution of conflicts, disarmament, and international cooperation in the pursuit of global peace and security.

India's Leadership in the Non-Aligned Movement: India emerged as a leading voice in the Non-Aligned Movement, leveraging its status as a newly independent nation and a champion of decolonization and anti-imperialism. Nehru's vision of non-alignment resonated with many developing countries seeking to assert their sovereignty and independence on the global stage. India hosted the first Non-Aligned Summit in 1961 in Belgrade and played a key role in shaping the movement's agenda and priorities, including disarmament, decolonization, and development.

Role in International Conflicts and Crises: India's non-aligned stance allowed it to play a constructive role in mediating conflicts and crises around the world, including the Suez Crisis, the Korean War, and the Cuban Missile Crisis. Nehru's policy of non-alignment enabled India to act as a mediator and bridge-builder between rival blocs, advocating for peaceful coexistence and dialogue. India's efforts in promoting disarmament, nuclear non-proliferation, and global peace earned it international acclaim and respect within the Non-Aligned Movement and beyond.

Legacy and Challenges: The Non-Aligned Movement played a significant role in shaping the global political landscape during the Cold War era, providing a platform for developing countries to assert their interests and influence on the world stage. However, the end of the Cold War and the emergence of new geopolitical realities posed challenges to the relevance and cohesion of the movement. In the post-Cold War era, India and other non-aligned countries have faced new challenges such as globalization, terrorism, and climate change, which require a renewed commitment to the principles of non-alignment and multilateralism.

Challenges of economic development, agrarian reforms, and the rise of regional parties

Economic Development Challenges:

a. Legacy of Colonialism: India inherited a largely agrarian economy from colonial rule, characterized by poverty, underdevelopment, and dependence on agriculture. The challenge of economic development was compounded by the need to address structural imbalances, inequalities, and disparities inherited from the colonial era.

b. Industrialization and Infrastructure: The process of industrialization and infrastructure development was hampered by resource constraints, inadequate technology, and bureaucratic inefficiency. The lack of investment in key sectors such as manufacturing, infrastructure, and technology hindered India's ability to achieve sustained economic growth and development.

c. Balance of Payments Crisis: India faced recurring balance of payments crises in the 1960s and 1970s, due to factors such as over-reliance on imports, declining exports, and external debt burden. The crisis highlighted the need for economic reforms, liberalization, and diversification of the economy to reduce dependence on foreign aid and assistance.

Agrarian Reforms:

a. Land Ownership Patterns: Agrarian reforms aimed at addressing inequalities in land ownership and distribution were a key priority for India's policymakers. The dominance of landlords, absentee landlords, and intermediaries in rural areas perpetuated landlessness, tenancy, and exploitation of small and marginal farmers. Agrarian reforms sought to redistribute land to landless peasants, promote tenant rights, and improve agricultural productivity.

b. Green Revolution: The Green Revolution of the 1960s and 1970s aimed at increasing agricultural productivity through the adoption of high-yielding varieties of seeds, modern agricultural techniques, and irrigation facilities. While the Green Revolution led to a significant increase in food production and self-sufficiency in staple crops such as wheat and rice, it also exacerbated disparities between regions, farmers, and social groups.

c. Challenges of Small Farmers: Small and marginal farmers faced numerous challenges, including access to credit, technology, markets, and infrastructure. The lack of institutional support, price volatility, and vulnerability to natural disasters further marginalized small-scale agriculture and contributed to rural poverty and distress.

Rise of Regional Parties:

a. Linguistic and Cultural Diversity: India's linguistic, ethnic, and cultural diversity gave rise to regional identities and aspirations, which found expression in the form of regional political parties. Regional parties emerged as vehicles for articulating regional grievances, promoting regional autonomy, and safeguarding cultural and linguistic rights.

b. Federalism and Decentralization: India's federal structure and system of governance provided opportunities for regional parties to assert their influence and demand a greater say in decision-making. The devolution of powers to states and the emergence of coalition politics at the national level facilitated the rise of regional parties as key players in India's political landscape.

c. Fragmentation of Political Mandate: The rise of regional parties led to increased fragmentation of the political mandate, with power becoming decentralized across multiple states and regions. While regional parties contributed to the deepening of democracy and representation, they also posed challenges of coalition politics, instability, and governance at the national level.

CHAPTER THREE

The Era of Coalition Politics (1964-1984)

The decline of the Congress dominance and the emergence of coalition politics

The Split in the Congress:

After Nehru's death in 1964, the Congress Party experienced internal rifts, leading to a split in 1969. This split resulted in the formation of two factions: the Congress (O), led by Morarji Desai, and the Congress (R), led by Indira Gandhi.

Indira Gandhi's faction, Congress (R), eventually became known as the Indian National Congress (Indira) or simply the Congress (I).

Indira Gandhi's Rise to Power:

Indira Gandhi's tenure as Prime Minister was marked by her populist policies and centralization of power.

She implemented several socialist reforms, such as nationalization of banks and abolition of privy purses, aiming to reduce economic inequality.

The Declaration of Emergency:

In 1975, facing political and legal challenges, Indira Gandhi declared a state of Emergency, suspending civil liberties and arresting opposition leaders.

The period of Emergency witnessed widespread censorship, forced sterilizations, and human rights abuses, leading to a backlash against the Congress Party.

Rise of Opposition Forces:

The imposition of Emergency led to a united opposition against the Congress Party.

Parties like the Janata Party, a coalition of anti-Congress forces, emerged as a viable alternative, leading to the defeat of the Congress in the 1977 general elections.

Coalition Politics:

The era following the Janata Party's victory saw the fragmentation of the political landscape, with the Congress no longer enjoying single-party dominance.

Regional parties gained prominence, particularly in states like Tamil Nadu, Andhra Pradesh, and West Bengal, challenging the hegemony of national parties.

Coalitions became the norm at the center, with no single party able to secure a clear majority in many elections.

Role of Regional Parties:

Regional parties played a crucial role in coalition politics, often holding the balance of power.

Leaders like M.G. Ramachandran (AIADMK), N.T. Rama Rao (Telugu Desam Party), and Jyoti Basu (Communist Party of India-Marxist) emerged as influential figures in their respective regions.

Legacy of Coalition Politics:

The period of coalition politics brought both opportunities and challenges for governance in India.

While it ensured greater representation for diverse voices and regions, it also led to issues of instability, policy paralysis, and frequent realignments of political alliances

The Split in the Congress

The Indian National Congress, founded in 1885, played a pivotal role in India's struggle for independence and emerged as the dominant political force post-independence. However, internal dissent and ideological differences within the party eventually led to a significant split in 1969, altering the course of Indian politics.

Background:

The Indian National Congress (INC) emerged as the vanguard of India's independence movement under the leadership of stalwarts like Mahatma Gandhi, Jawaharlal Nehru, Sardar Patel, and others. After India gained independence from British rule in 1947, the Congress Party became the dominant political force, securing overwhelming victories in the general elections.

However, despite its initial unity, the Congress Party began to experience internal fissures and ideological divisions. These fault lines became increasingly apparent following the death of Jawaharlal Nehru, the first Prime Minister of independent India, in 1964. Nehru's demise left a leadership vacuum within the party and exposed simmering disagreements over its future direction.

Key issues contributing to the internal turmoil within the Congress Party included:

Ideological Differences:

The Congress Party comprised members with diverse ideological leanings, ranging from socialist to conservative.

While some leaders advocated for socialist policies emphasizing state intervention in the economy and social welfare programs, others favored a more market-oriented approach and greater emphasis on individual freedoms.

Leadership Succession:

With Nehru's passing, the question of leadership succession became a contentious issue within the party.

Senior leaders like Morarji Desai, Lal Bahadur Shastri, and others harbored ambitions for the Prime Ministerial post, leading to intense rivalries and power struggles.

Economic Policies:

The Congress Party grappled with divergent views on economic policies, particularly regarding the role of the state versus the private sector.

While some leaders advocated for the nationalization of key industries and banks to promote economic equity, others favored a more laissez-faire approach to stimulate growth and investment.

Social Justice:

The issue of social justice, including caste-based discrimination and land reforms, also fueled internal debates within the party.

Leaders like Indira Gandhi championed populist measures aimed at empowering marginalized communities and addressing rural poverty, while others prioritized economic modernization and industrialization.

Against this backdrop of ideological divergence and leadership contention, the split in the Congress Party in 1969 emerged as a culmination of long-standing tensions. The rift not only altered the political landscape of India but also reshaped the trajectory of the Congress Party itself, setting the stage for a new era of coalition politics and ideological pluralism in Indian democracy.

Leadership Rift in the Congress Party:

The leadership rift within the Congress Party during the 1960s, particularly after the death of Jawaharlal Nehru, marked a critical period in Indian political history. This period was characterized by intense power struggles, ideological clashes, and personal ambitions among senior party leaders, ultimately leading to a significant split in the party in 1969. Here's a detailed exploration of the leadership rift:

Nehru's Legacy:

Jawaharlal Nehru, as the first Prime Minister of independent India, enjoyed immense popularity and held a central position within the Congress Party.

Nehru's visionary leadership and commitment to democratic ideals helped solidify the party's dominance in Indian politics during the early years of independence.

Leadership Vacuum:

Nehru's death in 1964 created a leadership vacuum within the Congress Party, as there was no clear successor to his charismatic leadership.

The absence of a designated heir apparent triggered speculation and uncertainty among party members regarding the future course of leadership.

Factionalism and Rivalries:

In the absence of Nehru's unifying presence, factionalism and rivalries among senior party leaders intensified.

Morarji Desai, Lal Bahadur Shastri, and others harbored aspirations for the Prime Ministerial post, leading to competing power centers within the party.

Personal ambitions and differing ideological orientations further fueled tensions and divisions among party members.

Ideological Disputes:

The leadership rift was exacerbated by ideological disputes within the Congress Party, particularly regarding economic policies and governance strategies.

While some leaders favored socialist-oriented policies, advocating for state intervention in the economy and social welfare programs, others espoused more conservative, market-oriented approaches.

These ideological differences deepened the rift within the party and contributed to the fragmentation of its leadership.

Emergence of Indira Gandhi:

Amidst the leadership vacuum and internal strife, Indira Gandhi, Nehru's daughter, emerged as a prominent figure within the Congress Party.

Gandhi's populist appeal and promise of bold reforms resonated with grassroots workers and sections of the party's base, catapulting her to prominence within the party hierarchy.

Split and Formation of Congress (R) and Congress (O):

The culmination of the leadership rift came in 1969 when the Congress Party split into two factions during a contentious session in Bombay (now Mumbai).

The faction led by Indira Gandhi retained control over the original Congress Party and came to be known as Congress (R), with 'R' standing for "requisition."

Morarji Desai and other dissenting members formed their faction known as Congress (O), with 'O' representing "organization."

Legacy and Impact:

The split in the Congress Party marked a significant turning point in Indian politics, signaling the end of the party's monolithic dominance and the beginning of a more fragmented political landscape.

It also set the stage for the emergence of coalition politics, regional parties, and ideological pluralism in Indian democracy.

The leadership rift underscored the challenges of leadership succession and the complexities of managing a diverse and ideologically disparate political organization.

Nationalization Policies:

Nationalization refers to the process by which the government takes control of privately-owned assets or industries, typically with the aim of achieving specific economic or social objectives. In the context of India in 1969, nationalization policies centered around the decision of Prime Minister Indira Gandhi to bring fourteen major commercial banks under state ownership and control. This move aimed to assert greater social control over the economy and reshape the banking sector in alignment with the government's developmental agenda. Here's a detailed exploration of the nationalization policies:

Background and Rationale:

In the 1960s, India was undergoing significant socio-economic transformation, with efforts focused on achieving economic self-reliance and reducing disparities inherited from colonial rule.

The banking sector, dominated by a few powerful private institutions, was perceived as playing a crucial role in shaping the country's economic trajectory.

Prime Minister Indira Gandhi and her advisors advocated for greater state intervention in key sectors of the economy as part of a broader strategy to promote social justice, economic equity, and planned development.

Objectives of Nationalization:

The decision to nationalize banks was driven by multiple objectives, including:

Broadening access to banking services, especially in rural and underserved areas.

Mobilizing financial resources for priority sectors such as agriculture, small-scale industries, and infrastructure development.

Mitigating the influence of powerful industrialists and promoting a more equitable distribution of credit.

Strengthening the role of the state in guiding economic policy and fostering development in line with socialist principles.

Implementation:

On July 19, 1969, the Indian government announced the nationalization of fourteen major private banks, accounting for approximately 85% of the banking sector's total assets.

The banks were effectively brought under government control through the issuance of an ordinance followed by parliamentary legislation.

The government acquired a majority stake in these banks, assuming control over their management, operations, and strategic decision-making processes.

The move was met with a mix of support and criticism from various quarters, with proponents lauding it as a bold step towards economic empowerment and opponents decrying it as a form of state overreach and interference in the free market.

Opposition and Criticism:

Nationalization policies faced stiff opposition, particularly from within the Congress Party itself.

Senior leaders like Morarji Desai, Lal Bahadur Shastri, and others voiced their dissent, arguing that nationalization would stifle entrepreneurship, hinder efficiency, and undermine the autonomy of the banking sector.

Critics raised concerns about bureaucratic inefficiencies, politicization of banking operations, and the potential erosion of investor confidence in the banking system.

Legacy and Impact:

The nationalization of banks left a lasting imprint on India's economic landscape, reshaping the contours of the banking sector and influencing the trajectory of economic policy.

While the move was hailed by many as a landmark initiative to promote financial inclusion and social justice, its long-term impact on economic efficiency, innovation, and competitiveness remains subject to debate.

Nationalization policies also served as a catalyst for political upheaval, contributing to the split within the Congress Party in 1969 and the emergence of new ideological fault lines within Indian politics.

Congress (O) and Congress (R):

Following the split in the Congress Party in 1969, two rival factions emerged: Congress (O) and Congress (R). These factions, led by Morarji Desai and Indira Gandhi respectively, represented divergent ideological orientations and leadership styles. Here's a detailed exploration of Congress (O) and Congress (R):

Congress (O):

Formation and Leadership:

Congress (O), also known as Congress (Organization), was formed by senior leaders who opposed Prime Minister Indira Gandhi's leadership and the policies of the Congress (R).

The faction was led by Morarji Desai, a veteran Congressman and former Deputy Prime Minister of India.

Desai, known for his austere lifestyle and pro-market economic views, emerged as the primary challenger to Indira Gandhi's leadership within the party.

Ideological Orientation:

Congress (O) espoused a more centrist and market-oriented approach to governance and economic policy.

Morarji Desai and his supporters advocated for liberalization, deregulation, and greater emphasis on individual freedoms and entrepreneurship.

The faction critiqued the socialist policies of Congress (R), arguing that they stifled economic growth, innovation, and private initiative.

Political Agenda:

Congress (O) positioned itself as a counterforce to the centralizing tendencies of Congress (R) and sought to uphold principles of democratic decentralization and institutional integrity.

Desai and his supporters emphasized the need for transparency, accountability, and good governance in public administration.

The faction also championed civil liberties, media freedom, and the rule of law as essential pillars of a vibrant democracy.

Electoral Performance:

Congress (O) contested elections against Congress (R) and other political parties, aiming to provide voters with an alternative to the ruling dispensation.

While the faction enjoyed pockets of support in certain regions, particularly among urban middle-class voters and business communities, it struggled to dislodge Congress (R) from power at the national level.

Congress (R):

Formation and Leadership:

Congress (R), also known as Congress (Requisition), was the faction led by Prime Minister Indira Gandhi and her supporters.

Following the split in the Congress Party, Indira Gandhi retained control over the original party structure and continued to lead Congress (R).

Ideological Orientation:

Congress (R) embraced a more socialist and interventionist approach to governance and economic policy.

Indira Gandhi advocated for the nationalization of key industries, land reforms, and social welfare programs aimed at reducing poverty and inequality.

The faction positioned itself as a champion of the poor and marginalized sections of society, emphasizing the role of the state in promoting social justice and equitable development.

Electoral Dominance:

Congress (R) enjoyed considerable electoral success during its tenure, winning consecutive elections and securing a dominant position in Indian politics.

Indira Gandhi's populist measures and mass appeal helped cement Congress (R)'s electoral dominance, despite growing opposition from rival parties and factions.

Political Ramifications of the Split in the Congress Party:

The split in the Congress Party in 1969 had far-reaching political ramifications that reshaped the landscape of Indian politics. The emergence of two rival factions, Congress (O) and Congress (R), and the subsequent realignment of political forces had profound implications for governance, electoral dynamics, and the broader trajectory of Indian democracy. Here's a detailed exploration of the political ramifications:

Fragmentation of Political Power:

The split in the Congress Party marked the end of its long-standing dominance as a monolithic political force in India.

With the emergence of two competing factions, political power became decentralized, leading to the fragmentation of the political landscape.

Regional parties and smaller political formations gained significance as alternatives to the Congress Party, contributing to the diversification of political representation at the national and state levels.

Rise of Coalition Politics:

The split in the Congress Party paved the way for the rise of coalition politics in India.

Neither Congress (O) nor Congress (R) could secure a clear majority in many elections, necessitating alliances with smaller parties and regional players to form governments.

Coalition governments became the norm at the center, ushering in an era of multi-party cooperation, negotiation, and compromise in governance.

Ideological Polarization:

The split deepened ideological fault lines within Indian politics, with Congress (O) and Congress (R) representing divergent visions for the country's future.

Congress (O) espoused a more centrist and market-oriented approach, advocating for liberalization, deregulation, and individual freedoms.

In contrast, Congress (R) embraced socialist policies and populist measures under Indira Gandhi's leadership, positioning itself as a champion of the poor and marginalized.

Electoral Competition:

The split intensified electoral competition among political parties, leading to a more competitive political environment.

Congress (O) and Congress (R) competed fiercely in elections, vying for the support of voters across the country.

The emergence of rival factions within the Congress Party also provided opportunities for other political parties to expand their influence and challenge the Congress hegemony.

Leadership Dynamics:

The split in the Congress Party reshuffled the deck of leadership dynamics within Indian politics.

While Indira Gandhi retained control over Congress (R) and continued to wield significant influence, Morarji Desai and other leaders of Congress (O) emerged as formidable opponents, challenging her leadership and policies.

The rivalry between these factions shaped the political discourse and decision-making processes, influencing policy directions and governance strategies.

Legacy of Factionalism:

The split in the Congress Party left a lasting legacy of factionalism and internal divisions within the party.

Subsequent leaders and factions within the Congress Party grappled with the legacy of the split, as ideological differences and leadership rivalries continued to shape its internal dynamics.

The Congress Party's struggle to reconcile these internal divisions and present a unified front had implications for its electoral performance and political relevance in the post-split era.

Impact on Indian Politics:

The split in the Congress Party in 1969 had a profound and enduring impact on Indian politics, shaping the trajectory of governance, electoral dynamics, and the broader socio-political landscape. Here's a detailed exploration of the impact of the split:

Fragmentation of Political Power:

The split marked the end of the Congress Party's hegemony as a dominant political force in India.

With the emergence of two rival factions, political power became decentralized, leading to the rise of regional parties and smaller political formations.

The era following the split witnessed increased competition among political parties, as new players entered the fray, challenging the traditional dominance of the Congress Party.

Rise of Coalition Politics:

The split paved the way for the rise of coalition politics in India, as neither Congress (O) nor Congress (R) could secure a clear majority in many elections.

Coalition governments became the norm at the center, with parties forming alliances to gain a majority and form governments.

The era of coalition politics brought greater representation for diverse voices and regions, but also posed challenges of stability and governance.

Deepening of Ideological Fault Lines:

The split deepened ideological fault lines within Indian politics, with Congress (O) and Congress (R) representing distinct visions for the country's future.

Congress (O) espoused a more centrist and market-oriented approach, advocating for liberalization and deregulation.

Congress (R), under Indira Gandhi's leadership, embraced socialist policies and populist measures, positioning itself as a champion of the poor and marginalized.

Evolution of Leadership Dynamics:

The split reshaped the leadership dynamics within Indian politics, as leaders of Congress (O) and Congress (R) emerged as formidable opponents to each other.

While Indira Gandhi retained control over Congress (R) and continued to wield significant influence, Morarji Desai and other leaders of Congress (O) challenged her leadership and policies.

The rivalry between these factions influenced policy decisions, governance strategies, and electoral campaigns, shaping the political discourse for decades to come.

Legacy of Factionalism:

The split left a lasting legacy of factionalism and internal divisions within the Congress Party.

Subsequent leaders and factions within the Congress Party grappled with the legacy of the split, as ideological differences and leadership rivalries continued to shape its internal dynamics.

The Congress Party's struggle to reconcile these internal divisions and present a unified front had implications for its electoral performance and political relevance in the post-split era.

Democratization of Indian Politics:

The split contributed to the democratization of Indian politics, as power became more decentralized and distributed among multiple political parties.

Regional parties gained prominence, especially in states where identity politics and regional aspirations played a significant role.

The era following the split witnessed greater political participation and representation for marginalized communities, women, and other historically underrepresented groups.

Indira Gandhi's Rise to Power:

Indira Gandhi, the daughter of Jawaharlal Nehru, India's first Prime Minister, rose to prominence in Indian politics in the wake of her father's death in 1964. Her journey to power was characterized by a combination of personal ambition, political maneuvering, and strategic decision-making. Here's a detailed exploration of Indira Gandhi's rise to power:

Background and Early Years:

Indira Gandhi was born on November 19, 1917, into a prominent political family. Her father, Jawaharlal Nehru, was a central figure in India's independence movement and served as Prime Minister for nearly seventeen years.

Growing up in the political milieu of the Indian National Congress, Indira was exposed to the ideals of nationalism, social justice, and democratic governance from an early age.

She received her education both in India and abroad, studying at institutions such as Somerville College, Oxford, where she developed a keen interest in politics and public affairs.

Entry into Politics:

Indira Gandhi's formal entry into politics came after her father's death in 1964, when she was appointed as a member of the Rajya Sabha, the upper house of India's Parliament.

Initially, she served as Minister of Information and Broadcasting in Lal Bahadur Shastri's cabinet, where she demonstrated her organizational skills and political acumen.

Ascendancy to Prime Ministership:

Indira Gandhi's ascendancy to the Prime Ministership came in 1966, following the sudden demise of Lal Bahadur Shastri. Despite initial skepticism from within the party due to her relative inexperience, she emerged as a consensus candidate.

As the leader of the Congress Party, Indira Gandhi positioned herself as a champion of the poor and marginalized, advocating for social justice and economic development.

Her populist policies and promises of bold reforms resonated with grassroots workers and sections of the party's base, catapulting her to power.

Centralization of Power:

Once in office, Indira Gandhi embarked on a path of centralization of power, consolidating control over key institutions and decision-making processes.

She marginalized potential rivals within the party and government, asserting her authority as the undisputed leader.

Indira Gandhi's leadership style was characterized by a mix of charisma, assertiveness, and pragmatism, as she navigated through political challenges and pursued her policy agenda.

Populist Policies and Socialist Reforms:

As Prime Minister, Indira Gandhi implemented a series of populist policies and socialist reforms aimed at addressing poverty, inequality, and social injustice.

Her government undertook measures such as nationalization of banks, abolition of privy purses, and land reforms to redistribute wealth and empower the poor.

Indira Gandhi's policies were often criticized for their authoritarian tendencies and economic inefficiencies but enjoyed broad support among certain sections of the population.

Challenges and Controversies:

Indira Gandhi's tenure as Prime Minister was marked by numerous challenges and controversies, including the declaration of Emergency in 1975, which saw the suspension of civil liberties and arrest of political opponents.

Her government faced criticism for its handling of various issues, including the Indo-Pakistani war of 1971, the Sikh separatist movement in Punjab, and allegations of corruption and nepotism.

Despite facing significant opposition and setbacks, Indira Gandhi remained a formidable political figure, adept at navigating through crises and maintaining her grip on power.

Legacy and Impact:

Indira Gandhi's legacy is a complex and contested one, characterized by her contributions to India's economic and social development, as well as her authoritarian tendencies and controversial decisions.

Her leadership left an indelible mark on Indian politics, shaping the trajectory of the country's governance, policy direction, and socio-political discourse.

While her rule was marked by both achievements and shortcomings, Indira Gandhi's tenure as Prime Minister remains a subject of intense scrutiny and debate, reflecting the complexities of leadership in a diverse and dynamic democracy.

The Declaration of Emergency:

In 1975, Indira Gandhi, then Prime Minister of India, declared a state of Emergency, marking one of the most controversial chapters in the country's democratic history. Faced with mounting political and legal challenges, Gandhi invoked emergency powers to suspend civil liberties, curtail fundamental rights, and consolidate authority. The period of Emergency, which lasted from June 25, 1975, to March 21, 1977, witnessed widespread censorship, political repression, forced sterilizations, and human rights abuses, leading to a severe backlash against the Congress Party. Here's a detailed exploration of the declaration of Emergency:

Political Context:

The decision to declare Emergency was precipitated by a series of political and legal challenges confronting Indira Gandhi's government.

In June 1975, the Allahabad High Court found Gandhi guilty of electoral malpractice during the 1971 general elections and invalidated her parliamentary seat.

Fearing imminent arrest and seeking to preempt further legal proceedings, Gandhi resorted to emergency powers enshrined in Article 352 of the Indian Constitution, which allowed the government to suspend civil liberties in the event of a national emergency.

Suspension of Civil Liberties:

The declaration of Emergency resulted in the suspension of fundamental rights guaranteed by the Constitution, including the right to freedom of speech, expression, and assembly.

Political opponents, activists, and journalists were detained under preventive detention laws, while civil liberties were curtailed through the imposition of strict censorship and media controls.

The government invoked draconian measures such as the Maintenance of Internal Security Act (MISA) and the Defense of India Rules (DIR) to suppress dissent and silence opposition voices.

Political Repression and Human Rights Abuses:

The period of Emergency witnessed widespread political repression, with opposition leaders, activists, and dissidents subjected to arbitrary arrests, torture, and harassment.

The government's crackdown extended beyond political opponents to include journalists, academics, and civil society activists critical of its policies.

Forced sterilizations, conducted under the guise of family planning programs, led to human rights abuses and violations of bodily autonomy, particularly among vulnerable communities.

Censorship and Media Controls:

Censorship was imposed on the press, cinema, literature, and other forms of expression, stifling freedom of speech and creativity.

Newspapers and magazines critical of the government were shut down or heavily censored, while journalists faced intimidation and harassment.

State-controlled media propagated government propaganda and suppressed dissenting voices, contributing to the erosion of democratic norms and public discourse.

Economic Reforms and Authoritarianism:

In addition to political repression, the government implemented economic policies aimed at centralizing control over key sectors of the economy.

Indira Gandhi's twenty-point program introduced sweeping reforms, including nationalization of banks, abolition of privy purses, and land reforms, consolidating state power and influence.

The period of Emergency witnessed a concentration of authority in the hands of the Prime Minister's Office, with Indira Gandhi exercising authoritarian control over governance and decision-making processes.

Backlash and Electoral Defeat:

The declaration of Emergency triggered widespread public outrage and resistance, both within India and internationally.

Opposition to the Congress Party's authoritarian rule coalesced around the Janata Party, a coalition of disparate political forces united in their commitment to restoring democracy and civil liberties.

In the 1977 general elections, held after the lifting of Emergency, the Congress Party suffered a resounding electoral defeat, with the Janata Party securing a landslide victory and forming the first non-Congress government at the center.

Rise of Opposition Forces:

The imposition of Emergency in 1975 under Prime Minister Indira Gandhi's government sparked a wave of dissent and resistance across India. The suspension of civil liberties, censorship, and political repression galvanized various opposition forces, ultimately leading to the emergence of a united front against the Congress Party. Among these opposition forces, the Janata Party, a coalition of anti-Congress parties, played a pivotal role in providing a viable alternative to the ruling regime. Here's a detailed exploration of the rise of opposition forces and the formation of the Janata Party:

Emergence of Opposition:

The imposition of Emergency triggered widespread public outrage and resistance, as citizens rallied against the Congress Party's authoritarian rule and suppression of civil liberties.

Political parties, activists, civil society groups, and ordinary citizens came together to oppose the Emergency and demand the restoration of democracy and fundamental rights.

The period of Emergency witnessed a resurgence of political activism and dissent, with opposition leaders and parties playing a key role in mobilizing public opinion against the government.

Formation of the Janata Party:

The Janata Party emerged as a coalition of diverse anti-Congress forces united in their commitment to restoring democracy, civil liberties, and accountable governance.

The party was formed through the merger of several opposition parties, including the Bharatiya Lok Dal, the Socialist Party, the Bharatiya Jana Sangh, and various regional parties.

Leaders such as Jayaprakash Narayan, Morarji Desai, Atal Bihari Vajpayee, and others played instrumental roles in the formation and leadership of the Janata Party.

Ideological Diversity:

The Janata Party comprised a wide spectru m of ideological orientations, ranging from socialists and liberals to conservatives and nationalists.

Despite their ideological differences, opposition leaders rallied around a common platform centered on the principles of democracy, secularism, and social justice.

The party's ideological diversity contributed to its broad appeal and ability to attract support from a cross-section of society.

Electoral Strategy:

In the run-up to the 1977 general elections, the Janata Party embarked on an ambitious electoral campaign aimed at mobilizing anti-Congress sentiment and presenting itself as a credible alternative.

The party capitalized on public discontent with the Congress Party's authoritarian rule and emphasized its commitment to restoring democratic norms and civil liberties.

The Janata Party's electoral strategy focused on forging alliances with regional parties, consolidating opposition votes, and projecting a united front against the Congress Party.

Landslide Victory in 1977:

The 1977 general elections, held after the lifting of Emergency, witnessed a historic landslide victory for the Janata Party.

The party secured a decisive mandate, winning a majority of seats in the Lok Sabha and forming the first non-Congress government at the center since independence.

Morarji Desai, a veteran leader and staunch opponent of the Emergency, was elected as Prime Minister, marking a significant political transition in Indian history.

Legacy and Impact:

The rise of the Janata Party and its electoral triumph in 1977 marked a watershed moment in Indian politics, signaling the resilience of democracy and the power of collective opposition.

The defeat of the Congress Party in the 1977 elections served as a stark reminder of the consequences of authoritarian rule and galvanized efforts to safeguard democratic institutions and values.

The Janata Party government, though short-lived and beset by internal divisions, implemented several reforms aimed at restoring democratic freedoms, promoting social justice, and fostering economic development

The Green Revolution

The Green Revolution refers to a series of agricultural initiatives and technological advancements implemented in

India during the 1960s and 1970s with the aim of increasing agricultural productivity and food grain production. It was a multi-faceted program that encompassed various elements, including the introduction of high-yielding varieties (HYVs) of seeds, increased use of fertilizers and pesticides, improved irrigation infrastructure, and agricultural extension services. Here's a detailed exploration of the Green Revolution:

Context and Background:

In the years following India's independence in 1947, the country faced severe food shortages and agricultural challenges, leading to periodic famines and widespread poverty.

The Green Revolution was launched in response to the urgent need to boost agricultural production and achieve food self-sufficiency to feed India's growing population.

Introduction of High-Yielding Varieties (HYVs):

The introduction of high-yielding varieties of seeds, developed through scientific research and breeding programs, formed the cornerstone of the Green Revolution.

HYVs of crops such as wheat, rice, and maize were characterized by their shorter growing periods, resistance to diseases, and higher yield potential compared to traditional varieties.

Expansion of Irrigation Infrastructure:

Another key component of the Green Revolution was the expansion and modernization of irrigation infrastructure, including the construction of dams, canals, and tube wells.

Access to reliable irrigation facilities helped mitigate the risks of drought and increased cropping intensity, allowing farmers to cultivate multiple crops in a single year.

Adoption of Modern Agricultural Practices:

The Green Revolution promoted the adoption of modern agricultural practices, including the use of chemical fertilizers, pesticides, and mechanized farm machinery.

These inputs, combined with improved seeds and irrigation, led to significant increases in crop yields and transformed agricultural productivity in regions where they were implemented.

Impact on Agricultural Production:

The Green Revolution had a transformative impact on agricultural production in India, particularly in regions like Punjab, Haryana, and parts of Uttar Pradesh.

Wheat and rice output witnessed substantial growth, leading to surplus production and reduced dependence on food imports.

The increase in agricultural productivity helped alleviate food scarcity, stabilize food prices, and improve rural livelihoods.

Nationalization of Banks:

The nationalization of banks in India refers to the process through which the government took control of major private banks and transformed them into public sector banks. This significant policy intervention, initiated in two phases in 1969 and 1980, aimed to achieve several socio-economic objectives, including expanding banking services, promoting financial inclusion, and directing credit to priority sectors. Here's a detailed exploration of the nationalization of banks:

Rationale and Objectives:

The nationalization of banks was driven by the government's commitment to socioeconomic development and its vision of a socialist-oriented mixed economy.

The primary objectives of nationalization were to mobilize savings, promote banking among rural and marginalized communities, and ensure equitable distribution of credit.

Phases of Nationalization:

The first phase of bank nationalization took place in 1969 under Prime Minister Indira Gandhi's government, wherein 14 major private banks were brought under state control.

The second phase occurred in 1980, during Indira Gandhi's second term as Prime Minister, when six more private banks were nationalized, further consolidating government ownership in the banking sector.

Expansion of Banking Services:

Nationalization led to a significant expansion of banking services, particularly in rural and underserved areas where private banks had limited presence.

Public sector banks were mandated to open branches in remote locations, provide basic banking facilities, and mobilize savings from rural households.

Priority Sector Lending:

Nationalized banks were directed to prioritize lending to sectors considered crucial for economic development, such as agriculture, small-scale industries, and exports.

The concept of priority sector lending aimed to channel credit to sectors that had historically been neglected by private banks, thereby promoting inclusive growth and addressing regional disparities.

Impact on Financial Inclusion:

The nationalization of banks played a significant role in expanding financial inclusion and increasing banking penetration across India.

Access to banking services, including savings accounts, loans, and insurance products, became more accessible to a broader segment of the population, especially in rural and semi-urban areas.

Criticisms and Challenges:

While nationalization helped achieve certain socio-economic objectives, it also faced criticism for its impact on efficiency, innovation, and autonomy in banking operations.

Public sector banks grappled with issues of bureaucratic red tape, political interference, and inefficiencies, leading to concerns about their competitiveness and performance.

Overall, the nationalization of banks in India represented a significant policy intervention aimed at promoting socioeconomic development and financial inclusion. While it achieved certain objectives, it also posed challenges that necessitated ongoing reforms and restructuring within the banking sector to address issues of efficiency, accountability, and sustainability.

The Mandal Commission:

The Mandal Commission, officially known as the Second Backward Classes Commission, was constituted by the Indian government in 1979 under the chairmanship of B.P. Mandal with the mandate to identify socially and educationally backward classes and recommend measures for their upliftment. The commission's report, submitted in 1980, recommended the reservation of 27% of government jobs and educational institution seats for Other Backward Classes (OBCs). Here's a detailed exploration of the Mandal Commission and its impact:

Background and Context:

The Mandal Commission was set up against the backdrop of growing demands for social justice and affirmative action to address the historical injustices faced by marginalized communities in India.

The commission's mandate was to identify and recommend measures for the advancement of socially and educationally backward classes, distinct from Scheduled Castes (SCs) and Scheduled Tribes (STs).

Identification of OBCs:

The Mandal Commission conducted an extensive survey and analysis to identify socially and educationally backward classes based on criteria such as social status, educational attainment, and economic indicators.

The commission classified communities into three categories: backward, more backward, and most backward, and recommended reservation benefits for OBCs in government jobs, educational institutions, and other sectors.

Implementation and Controversies:

The implementation of the Mandal Commission recommendations sparked widespread debates, protests, and political controversies across India.

Critics of the reservation policy argued that it would lead to reverse discrimination, undermine meritocracy, and create tensions among different social groups.

However, supporters of the Mandal Commission hailed it as a milestone in the struggle for social justice and empowerment of historically marginalized communities.

Impact on Politics and Society:

The Mandal Commission recommendations had far-reaching implications for Indian politics and society, reshaping electoral dynamics and mobilizing caste-based identities.

Political parties, particularly those representing OBC communities, sought to capitalize on the issue of reservation to mobilize support and consolidate their electoral base.

The implementation of reservation policies led to increased representation of OBCs in government institutions, public services, and educational institutions, fostering greater social inclusion and empowerment.

Challenges and Criticisms:

Despite its positive impact in addressing historical injustices and promoting social equity, the Mandal Commission faced criticisms and challenges in its implementation.

Issues such as inadequate representation of certain OBC communities, creamy layer exclusions, and challenges in determining backwardness criteria remained contentious and unresolved.

Continuing Relevance:

The Mandal Commission and the issue of reservation for OBCs continue to be relevant and contested in contemporary Indian politics.

Debates surrounding reservation policies, quotas, and affirmative action measures remain central to discussions on social justice, equality, and representation in Indian society.

CHAPTER FOUR

Liberalization and Economic Reforms (1984-2004)

Rajiv Gandhi's tenure and the beginning of economic liberalization:

Rajiv Gandhi assumed office as the Prime Minister of India following the tragic assassination of his mother, Indira Gandhi, in 1984. His tenure marked a period of significant transition, both in terms of economic policy and political landscape. Rajiv Gandhi embarked on a path of economic liberalization, initiating reforms aimed at modernizing India's economy, encouraging foreign investment, and fostering technological advancement. The period also witnessed the emergence of pressing socio-political issues, including the Babri Masjid demolition, Mandal Commission protests, and the rise of identity politics.

Economic Reforms under Rajiv Gandhi:

Rajiv Gandhi's tenure saw the initiation of economic reforms aimed at liberalizing India's economy and integrating it into the global market.

The government pursued policies aimed at reducing bureaucratic red tape, promoting entrepreneurship, and attracting foreign investment.

Initiatives such as the introduction of computerization, telecommunications reforms, and efforts to promote technological innovation signaled a shift towards a more modern and globally connected economy.

Technological Advancement and Modernization:

Rajiv Gandhi emphasized the importance of technological advancement and modernization as key drivers of economic growth and development.

His government launched the National Informatics Centre (NIC) and introduced policies to promote computer literacy and expand access to information technology (IT) services.

Efforts to harness the potential of IT and telecommunications laid the groundwork for India's emergence as a global hub for software services and technology outsourcing in subsequent years.

Socio-Political Challenges:

Despite the focus on economic reforms, Rajiv Gandhi's tenure was marred by various socio-political challenges that tested the fabric of Indian society.

The Babri Masjid demolition in 1992, followed by communal riots and sectarian violence, highlighted the deep-seated religious and communal tensions within the country.

The Mandal Commission protests, triggered by the implementation of reservations for Other Backward Classes (OBCs) in government jobs and educational institutions, fueled debates around caste-based identity politics and social justice.

Rise of Identity Politics:

The period from 1984 to 2004 witnessed the rise of identity politics, with various communities and interest groups asserting their political demands and aspirations.

Caste-based movements, such as the mobilization of OBCs under the Mandal Commission, challenged traditional power structures and reshaped electoral dynamics.

The emergence of regional parties representing linguistic, ethnic, and regional identities further fragmented the political landscape and reshaped the contours of Indian federalism.

Coalition Governments and Regional Parties:

The period saw the emergence of coalition governments at the center, reflecting the growing influence of regional parties and the decline of single-party dominance.

Regional parties, such as the Dravida Munnetra Kazhagam (DMK), Telugu Desam Party (TDP), and Samajwadi Party (SP), played crucial roles in coalition politics, often holding the balance of power.

Coalition governments faced challenges of stability and governance, as diverse political interests and ideological differences necessitated constant negotiation and compromise.

CHAPTER FIVE

Coalition Politics and Socio-Economic Transformations (2004-2014)

The period from 2004 to 2014 witnessed significant developments in Indian politics and socio-economic landscape, characterized by the continuation of coalition governments at the center, alongside notable socio-economic transformations. This chapter delves into the intricacies of coalition politics, key policy initiatives, and socio-economic changes that defined this era.

Coalition Governments and Political Dynamics:

Coalition politics continued to dominate the Indian political landscape during this period, with no single party able to secure a clear majority in the Lok Sabha.

The United Progressive Alliance (UPA), led by the Indian National Congress, formed the government at the center after the 2004 and 2009 general elections, relying on support from coalition partners.

The UPA government's tenure was marked by complex negotiations, compromises, and coalition management, as diverse political interests and regional parties wielded significant influence.

Economic Reforms and Policy Initiatives:

The period witnessed several significant economic reforms and policy initiatives aimed at promoting inclusive growth, fostering economic development, and addressing socio-economic challenges.

The UPA government implemented flagship programs such as the Mahatma Gandhi National Rural Employment Guarantee Act (MGNREGA), aimed at providing employment opportunities and enhancing rural livelihoods.

Initiatives such as the National Rural Health Mission (NRHM) and the National Rural Livelihood Mission (NRLM) were launched to improve healthcare services and empower rural communities.

Infrastructure Development and Urbanization:

The UPA government prioritized infrastructure development and urbanization as key drivers of economic growth and development.

Major infrastructure projects, including the Golden Quadrilateral highway network and the Jawaharlal Nehru National Urban Renewal Mission (JNNURM), were launched to improve connectivity, urban infrastructure, and quality of life in cities.

Investments in sectors such as transportation, energy, and telecommunications were aimed at enhancing India's competitiveness and attracting foreign investment.

Social Welfare Schemes and Inclusive Policies:

The UPA government introduced a range of social welfare schemes and inclusive policies aimed at addressing poverty, inequality, and social exclusion.

Programs such as the Right to Information Act (RTI), the National Rural Health Mission (NRHM), and the National Food Security Act (NFSA) were enacted to empower citizens, improve access to essential services, and ensure food security for vulnerable populations.

Efforts to expand access to education, healthcare, and social protection programs contributed to improvements in human development indicators and standards of living.

Challenges and Controversies:

Despite its achievements, the UPA government faced several challenges and controversies during its tenure.

Issues such as corruption scandals, policy paralysis, and governance failures tarnished the government's image and eroded public trust.

The government's handling of issues such as inflation, unemployment, and fiscal deficit came under scrutiny, leading to criticism from opposition parties and civil society.

Socio-Economic Transformations:

The period from 2004 to 2014 witnessed significant socio-economic transformations, driven by demographic changes, urbanization, and globalization.

India's economy experienced robust growth, with GDP expanding at an average rate of around 7-8% per year, leading to improvements in per capita income and living standards.

The emergence of a dynamic middle class, rapid urbanization, and the spread of information and communication technologies (ICTs) contributed to shifts in consumption patterns, lifestyles, and aspirations.

Globalization and Integration:

India's integration into the global economy deepened during this period, with increased trade, investment, and technological exchanges with the rest of the world.

The country's growing prominence on the global stage was reflected in its participation in international forums, negotiations on trade agreements, and collaborations in areas such as climate change and sustainable development.

CHAPTER SIX

Political Shifts and Socio-Economic Challenges (2014-2024)

The period from 2014 to 2024 was characterized by significant political shifts, transformative policy initiatives, and persistent socio-economic challenges in India. This chapter delves into the intricacies of the evolving political landscape, key policy developments, and the complex socio-economic dynamics that defined this era.

Political Landscape and Electoral Dynamics:

The Bharatiya Janata Party (BJP), led by Narendra Modi, secured a historic victory in the 2014 general elections, forming a majority government at the center.

The BJP's victory marked a significant shift in India's political landscape, signaling the emergence of a dominant national party with a strong mandate for governance.

The Modi government's tenure was marked by bold policy initiatives, proactive diplomacy, and efforts to promote economic growth and development.

Economic Reforms and Policy Initiatives:

The Modi government launched several ambitious economic reforms and policy initiatives aimed at promoting growth, enhancing competitiveness, and fostering inclusive development.

Initiatives such as Make in India, Digital India, and Startup India were launched to promote manufacturing, digitalization, and entrepreneurship, aimed at creating jobs and stimulating economic growth.

The introduction of the Goods and Services Tax (GST) in 2017 represented a significant tax reform aimed at streamlining India's indirect tax system and promoting ease of doing business.

Socio-Economic Challenges and Reforms:

Despite efforts to promote economic growth and development, India continued to grapple with persistent socio-economic challenges during this period.

Issues such as poverty, unemployment, inequality, and agrarian distress remained significant concerns, necessitating targeted policy interventions and reforms.

The government launched schemes such as the Pradhan Mantri Jan Dhan Yojana (PMJDY), Pradhan Mantri Fasal Bima Yojana (PMFBY), and Ayushman Bharat to address financial inclusion, agricultural insurance, and healthcare access, respectively.

Infrastructural Development and Urbanization:

The Modi government prioritized infrastructural development and urbanization as key pillars of economic growth and modernization.

Initiatives such as the Smart Cities Mission, Housing for All, and the Atal Mission for Rejuvenation and Urban Transformation (AMRUT) aimed to improve urban infrastructure, housing, and quality of life in cities.

Investments in transportation, energy, and digital infrastructure were made to enhance connectivity, efficiency, and productivity.

Foreign Policy and International Relations:

The Modi government pursued an assertive foreign policy aimed at strengthening India's position on the global stage and enhancing its strategic partnerships.

Efforts were made to deepen economic engagement with major powers, attract foreign investment, and promote India's interests in multilateral forums.

Initiatives such as the Act East Policy, Neighbourhood First Policy, and Indo-Pacific Strategy underscored India's commitment to regional integration and security cooperation.

Challenges and Controversies:

The period from 2014 to 2024 was marked by controversies, challenges, and debates surrounding various policy decisions and governance issues.

Controversies such as the demonetization of high-denomination currency notes in 2016 and the implementation of the Citizenship Amendment Act (CAA) in 2019 sparked widespread debate and criticism.

The government faced challenges related to job creation, social tensions, environmental degradation, and healthcare infrastructure, highlighting the complexities of governance in a diverse and rapidly changing society.

Resilience and Adaptation:

Despite facing challenges, India demonstrated resilience and adaptability in navigating socio-economic changes and global uncertainties during this period.

The country's robust democratic institutions, vibrant civil society, and entrepreneurial spirit contributed to its ability to weather challenges and capitalize on opportunities.

Innovations in technology, entrepreneurship, and governance showcased India's potential for transformation and emergence as a global leader in the 21st century.

CHAPTER SEVEN

Corruption and Politicians

It's difficult to guarantee that any politician is completely free from corruption, there are certainly individuals who have demonstrated a strong commitment to integrity, transparency, and public service throughout their careers. These politicians prioritize the well-being of their constituents over personal gain and adhere to ethical principles in their conduct.

As for the possibility of a politician managing an entire country by always listening to the public, it's essential to recognize the complexities of governance and decision-making in a diverse and populous nation like India. While public opinion and feedback are important considerations for policymakers, governance also requires expertise, foresight, and the ability to make difficult decisions in the best interest of the nation as a whole.

In a democratic setup like India, politicians are accountable to the electorate and must balance the competing interests and demands of various stakeholders, including the public, business leaders, civil society organizations, and other branches of government. Effective governance entails a delicate balance between responsiveness to public concerns and the pursuit of long-term national interests, often necessitating compromise and negotiation.

While it's challenging for any politician to fully satisfy every segment of the population, those who prioritize transparency, accountability, and inclusive decision-making can foster greater trust and legitimacy in the democratic process. Building robust institutions, promoting civic engagement, and combating corruption are essential steps towards ensuring effective and responsive governance in India and elsewhere.

CHAPTER EIGHT

Ideal qualities a politician should have

Ideal qualities for a politician can vary depending on the context and the demands of the position they hold. However, some universally valued qualities include:

Integrity: A politician should possess honesty, transparency, and ethical conduct. Integrity builds trust among constituents and enhances the credibility of political leaders.

Leadership: Effective leadership entails the ability to inspire, motivate, and guide others toward common goals. A politician should demonstrate vision, decisiveness, and the capacity to navigate complex challenges.

Accountability: Politicians should be accountable to the people they represent, taking responsibility for their actions, decisions, and promises. Being answerable to constituents fosters transparency and strengthens democratic governance.

Empathy: Empathy involves understanding and compassion for the experiences, concerns, and perspectives of others. Politicians who demonstrate empathy can better represent the diverse needs and interests of their constituents.

Communication Skills: Effective communication is essential for a politician to convey ideas, engage with constituents, and negotiate with stakeholders. Clear, persuasive communication fosters transparency, collaboration, and public trust.

Problem-Solving Ability: Politicians should possess critical thinking skills and the capacity to analyze complex issues, identify solutions, and make evidence-based decisions. Problem-solving skills are essential for addressing the diverse challenges facing society.

Respect for Diversity: Respect for diversity entails valuing and embracing the differences in culture, religion, ethnicity, gender, and socio-economic background. Politicians should promote inclusivity, tolerance, and social cohesion in their actions and policies.

Commitment to Public Service: True public servants prioritize the well-being of the community over personal interests or partisan agendas. Politicians should demonstrate a genuine dedication to serving the public good and improving the lives of their constituents.

Adaptability: In a rapidly changing world, politicians must be adaptable and open to new ideas, perspectives, and approaches. Flexibility enables politicians to respond effectively to evolving challenges and opportunities.

Collaboration: Collaboration involves working constructively with colleagues, stakeholders, and across party lines to achieve common objectives. Politicians who prioritize collaboration can build consensus, foster bipartisanship, and advance collective interests.

Overall, politicians who embody these qualities are better equipped to lead with integrity, serve their constituents effectively, and contribute to the well-being and progress of society.

CHAPTER NINE

Prime Ministers of India from 1947 to 2022

Jawaharlal Nehru (1947–1964)

Gulzarilal Nanda (1964 and 1966; served as Acting
Prime Minister twice)

Lal Bahadur Shastri (1964–1966)

Indira Gandhi (1966–1977) &(1980–1984)

Morarji Desai (1977–1979)

Charan Singh (1979–1980)

Rajiv Gandhi (1984–1989)

Vishwanath Pratap Singh (1989–1990)

Chandra Shekhar (1990–1991)

P. V. Narasimha Rao (1991–1996)

Atal Bihari Vajpayee (1996; 1998–2004)

H. D. Deve Gowda (1996–1997)

Inder Kumar Gujral (1997–1998)

Manmohan Singh (2004–2014)

Narendra Modi (2014–present, as of 2024)

CHAPTER TEN

Conclusion

The journey through India's political evolution from 1947 to 2024 has been a complex tapestry woven with the threads of democracy, diversity, and development. As we conclude this exploration, it is evident that India has traversed through a myriad of challenges and triumphs, shaping its identity as one of the world's largest and most vibrant democracies.

From the early years of nation-building under the leadership of visionaries like Jawaharlal Nehru to the emergence of coalition politics and the economic reforms of the 1990s, India's political landscape has been dynamic and ever-evolving. The chapters of this book have unfolded the narratives of political upheavals, socio-economic transformations, and the resilience of the Indian spirit in the face of adversity.

Through the lens of history, we have witnessed the rise and fall of political giants, the emergence of new ideologies, and the forging of alliances that have shaped the course of governance. We have examined the impact of economic policies, such as the Green Revolution and liberalization, on the lives of millions, as well as the socio-political ramifications of initiatives like the Mandal Commission and nationalization of banks.

Amidst the ebbs and flows of politics, one constant has been the unwavering commitment to democracy and the rule of law. India's vibrant democratic institutions have served as the bedrock of stability and continuity, ensuring the peaceful transfer of power and providing avenues for citizens to participate in the democratic process.

As we look towards the future, it is imperative to acknowledge the challenges that lie ahead – from addressing socio-economic inequalities and environmental degradation to fostering inclusive growth and strengthening democratic institutions. The lessons gleaned from India's political journey offer valuable insights into the path forward.

In closing, let us recognize the resilience, diversity, and democratic ethos that define the essence of India. As the nation continues its journey of progress and development, let us draw inspiration from its rich tapestry of history and forge ahead with optimism, unity, and a steadfast commitment to building a better tomorrow for all its citizens.